Banana splits

ways into part-singing

Compiled and edited by Ana Sanderson

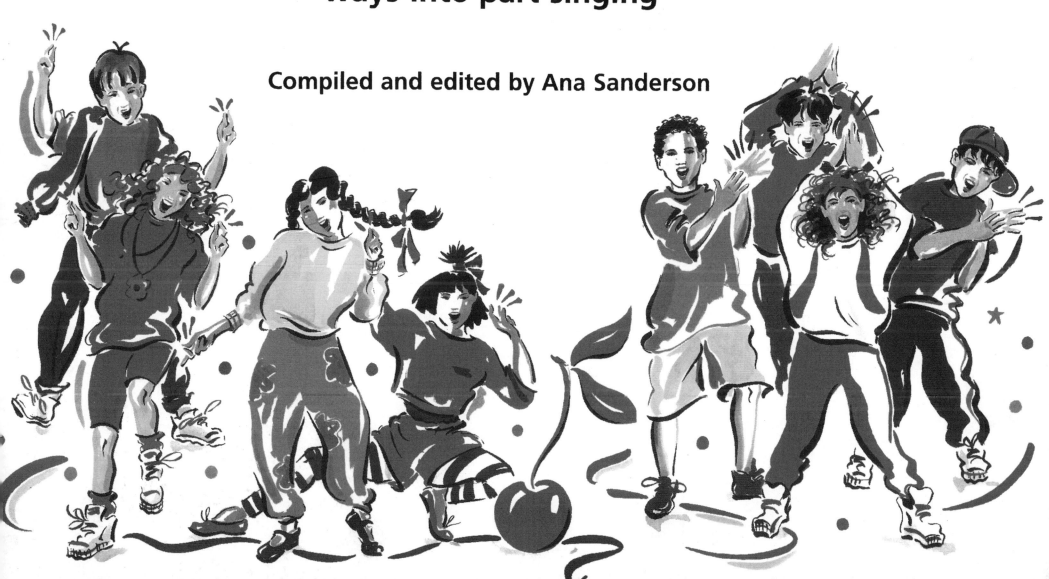

Contents

First published 1995
Published by Collins
An imprint of HarperCollins*Publishers* Ltd
The News Building
1 London Bridge Street
London
SE1 9GF
Reprinted 1996, 1998, 2001, 2003, 2008, 2012
Reprinted by Collins 2017
ISBN 978-0-7136-4196-7

Cover illustration by Connie Jude
Line drawings by Phil Dobson
Compiled and edited by Ana Sanderson
Music set by Andrew Jones
Designed by Dorothy Moir
Printed in Great Britain by Martins the Printers,
Berwick upon Tweed

This book is produced using paper that is made from wood grown in managed, sustainable forests. It is natural, renewable and recyclable. The logging and manufacturing processes conform to the environmental regulations of the country of origin.

After you
Rounds and canons

How fitting
Partner songs

Just desserts
Performance songs with independent parts

Tips for teaching

Part-singing is fun with Banana Splits

Everyone knows that children love singing! The songs in this book are intended for children who have already had opportunities to explore their voices through singing simple songs with other children, and are discovering how to use their voices in a more controlled way. Part-singing requires at least two people (or groups of people) to sing at least two different musical lines which fit together to make a song performance. The songs, chants and games included in this collection either involve simple part-singing or help to prepare children for part-singing at a later stage; the early songs can be attempted by children with any level of vocal ability.

It is important that your pupils work on singing accurately, clearly and uniformly in a group. These qualities, when singing, make it easier for two groups to sing two different parts at the same time. Children can learn and practise these qualities when singing, as they develop awareness of their voices.

When teaching a part-song, prepare yourself carefully before teaching it to your pupils. Consider each of the parts to be sung and look for the most suitable moments to breathe. Try to familiarise yourself with how the parts should sound together. Remember that unaccompanied songs can be sung at a higher or lower pitch to suit your pupils.

The various songs in 'Banana Splits' are described in the following sections. There are also ideas about what can be achieved or gained from doing part-singing. The tips for teachers give you helpful hints on how to introduce and teach the songs to children effectively.

Simple starters

Songs for keeping the beat going

It is important to be able to keep in time when part-singing and making music generally. If two groups of singers are singing two different lines together, the final effect will partly depend on both groups keeping in time with each other.

In order to keep in time, the pupils need to be aware of the pulse or beat in the music. The songs and chants in this section all focus on beat. 'Clap your hands' (p9) has amusing actions to perform in time to the instrumental interlude. 'Banana splits' (p8) has actions to be performed with words which are on the beat. And in 'Choo choo' (p10), the children make the regular 'choo choo' sound of a train.

When you ask your pupils to clap in time to a song, you may find that some children clap the rhythm of the melody instead of the beat. Actions with a natural pulse or beat, such as marching (if you have enough space) or swinging one's arms as though walking may help children feel the beat.

Tip for teaching
Teaching any songs while marking the beat.

When teaching a song, e.g. 'Choo choo' (p10), ask the children to clap or tap the beat as you sing or play the melody of the song.

| *clap* | *clap* | *clap* | *clap* |
| Once there was | a | choo | choo, |

| *clap* | *clap* | *clap* | *clap* |
| But he | couldn't | choo | choo, |

Teach the song, then ask the children to sing it while clapping in time with the beat. Think of other actions that the children can perform on the beat, such as tapping toes, patting knees and clicking fingers. Try them while singing the song.

The games in this section encourage children to learn to keep time and help teachers to identify any children who may need more help. In 'Traffic lights' (p12) and 'Jack-in-the-box' (p13) the children sing short sections of songs in their heads while keeping the beat of the song going. When you give the children the signal to sing out loud again, you can hear if everyone begins singing the same moment in the song.

It takes two!

Call and response, conversation and echo songs

To sing in parts successfully, your pupils need to be able to sing a part while listening to what another group sings. Call and response, conversation and echo songs provide excellent preparation for this as they are simple songs suitable for introducing children gently to the idea of listening **and** singing when performing. Each group of performers has a role in each song, such as being in a conversation, which should encourage them to listen to what the other group is singing.

The songs in this section provide excellent opportunities for continuing work on keeping in time. 'Mister Clicketty Cane' (p14) has a chorus in which the children can swing their arms in time to the beat and 'Have you ever?' (p20) is a conversation song with actions and clapping on the beat. Each group of children should try to sing its part of the conversation, echo or call and response without hesitating or rushing.

All the skills that can be practised through the songs in this section are reinforced in games such as 'Time for a hocket' (p22), 'Tambourine talk' (p26), and 'Jungle sounds' (p27).

Call and response songs require a leader (or group of leaders) and a chorus (a group). The response is usually a simple phrase which is sung after the leader's part.

Tip for teaching
Introducing call and response

Sing both parts of a call and response song such as 'Ewe!' (pronounced Eh-weh) on p18, to your pupils. Sing it again and ask everyone to join in with the chorus part (part 2). If necessary, give a signal to show when the pupils should sing.

Teach everyone the leader's part (part 1). This may take some time. When everyone can sing it confidently, ask them to perform the leader's part while you sing the response part.

Most songs can be taught by asking your pupils to echo what you sing and because echoing involves listening and copying, children can improve their ability to repeat a musical phrase accurately. Songs with echoes are easy to teach because everyone sings the same line but at different times.

Tip for teaching
Introducing songs with echoes.

Teach a song with echoes, e.g. 'Mister Clicketty Cane' (p15), verses only. Tell your pupils to copy what you sing after you've sung it. If necessary, use hand signals to show when they should begin to sing. Sing part 1. The children who are echoing are effectively singing part 2.

When the children are familiar with the verses, ask them to sing part 1. They may need prompting at first. You sing the echo (part 2). Then divide the children into two groups to sing the verses.

In most songs in this section, the two groups of performers sing at different times. However, echo songs like 'Tongo' (p25) provide opportunities to hear two groups singing at once, as each group holds the last note of its phrase on while the other group sings its next line. This gives children a chance to try performing and listening at the same time with a simple song. 'Sing a little song' (p16) can be introduced as written (with the groups singing one at a time), then developed in this way. Again, remember that everyone must keep in time. The group beginning while the other group holds on its last note should not hesitate or rush.

Before teaching a conversation song, consider the song as a whole as well as the individual parts.

Tip for teaching
Teaching conversation songs with no overlapping parts.

Teach a song, such as 'I hear the bells' (p23) as a whole song (one tune sung by everyone) until everyone is familiar with it. Then divide the pupils into two separate groups and allocate the parts.

A chant like 'TV tantrum' (p26) has moments at which both groups perform at once. Both groups must keep in time with each other.

Over and over
Songs with ostinato parts

A phrase or pattern of notes repeated over and over again is called an ostinato. The songs in this section contain second parts with short action patterns, rhythms or tunes which are repeated over and over again.

The ostinato parts are quick and easy to teach because the phrase to be repeated over and over again is usually short and memorable. However, it is important not to rush or hesitate when performing an ostinato. 'Four white horses' (p31) has an ostinato clapping pattern on the beat throughout. Either divide the children into two groups, one singing, one clapping, or ask everyone to sing and perform the ostinato clapping pattern at the same time.

You should prepare for teaching a song with an ostinato part by looking at how each part sounds by itself, and how the two parts fit together to make a complete performance. Look for moments where the ostinato part and melody part are similar or different. This will help you when you teach or rehearse the song. Try to develop your listening skills so that you are aware of how the song should sound, can hear how it actually sounds, and deal with any problems which might arise in rehearsal.

Tip for teaching
Introducing songs with sung ostinato parts

Teach the ostinato part of a song like 'I love the flowers' (p35), while clapping or tapping a steady beat. Suggest a good moment in the music to breathe. When the children can perform the ostinato part confidently without rushing or hesitating, sing or play the song melody.

When you join in with the song melody, the children may stop singing because they are distracted. When they get used to the idea of singing at the same time as you, they may rush or hesitate as they sing their part. Ideally they should adjust their volume in order to listen to the song melody while they sing the ostinato part and keep in time. Ask them what they noticed about their singing and your singing or playing.

Teach everyone the song melody while clapping or tapping a beat to keep in time. When the children can sing it confidently, play or sing the ostinato part at the same time. You should aim to help the children keep time when performing, while being aware of the other part. Then divide the children into two groups to sing both parts at the same time.

'More jungle sounds' (p30), 'Beat box' (p32), and 'Make up your own ostinato (1)' (p30) provide opportunites to make up ostinatos that can be played or sung along with other parts. 'Parade day!' (p32) is a game which helps children keep time while chanting an ostinato.

Songs with several ostinato parts, such as 'The band' (p38), provide wonderful opportunities for exploring dynamics (loudness and quietness) and balance (how loud or quiet each part should be in relation to the other). Ask your pupils if each group can hear the other group when they sing. Explore what happens when one group sings very loudly and the other sings very quietly. Ask the children to consider which part is the most interesting to listen to, and therefore which part should be loudest. (In general, the melody should be louder than the ostinato for a satisfying effect.)

After you
Rounds and canons

A round or canon is a tune that fits with itself when sung by at least two people beginning at different times. Rounds can usually be accompanied by a simple harmony which repeats over and over again. However, the harmony in a canon can change and develop. Rounds may have two, three or four parts whereas as a canon usually has two parts. Rounds and canons are easy and fun to teach because everyone begins by learning the melody as a simple song sung together. When your pupils are familiar and confident with the melody, divide them into groups to make the song into a round or canon.

For rounds or canons to be successful, the second, third and fourth groups must begin singing the melody at the correct moment, while everyone keeps in time. Clap or tap the beat when teaching the melody and when singing the song as a round. This will help the children to keep in time.

The moments at which the second group (and third and fourth groups) begins to sing are called entry points. They are marked * in the music. When the first group reaches the * shown in the music, the second group begins.

Tip for teaching
Practising round and canon entry points

Sing from the beginning of a song, such as 'Autumn leaves' (p40), up to the asterisk shown in the music. Ask the pupils to echo what you sing. Make sure that your pupils do not hesitate before singing the echo.

Teacher: Autumn leaves are falling,
Pupils: Autumn leaves are falling,

When your pupils have done this successfully, do it again. This time, when the pupils echo, you continue singing the next line of the song.

'Noah's shanty' (p49) has two possible entry points for the second part. Teach both entry points separately in the above way.

Ostinatos can be performed effectively with rounds - suitable ostinatos are suggested with some songs.

How fitting
Partner songs

Partner songs are two different songs which fit together when sung at the same time. They are fun to teach because everyone gets to learn a whole song. Some songs in this section like 'God bless the master' (p56) and 'Mums and Dads' (p58) have sections which can be sung at the same time.

The tip for teachers below is particularly suitable for 'London Bridge/Pease pudding hot' (p51), 'Alleluia Amen/Michael, row the boat ashore' (p54) and 'Ten green bottles/Green glass' (p51).

Before teaching the partner songs, look for any moments when both groups sing something different or something similar. Also look for suitable moments for each group to breathe.

Tip for teaching
Introducing partner songs

Teach your pupils the lesser-known or more difficult partner song. Clap or tap the beat as you sing it. As everyone sings it confidently, you join in playing or singing the other partner song. Your pupils may stop or hesitate in order to listen to you. Ask them to carry on singing in time, but to sing quietly enough to hear what you sing. Ask the children what they noticed during the sing-through. Then teach the other song and divide the pupils into two groups to sing the songs as partner songs.

Make sure that both groups know how to find their starting notes. You can play a short introduction, then the first note of each partner song. Check whether both songs begin at the same time. In 'Alleluia amen/Michael, row the boat ashore' (p54), group 2 begin two beats before group 1.

Just desserts
Performance songs with independent parts

Most songs in this section feature at least one aspect or skill practised in the previous sections in this book. The verse of 'Wipe, sniff, drip', (p60), is an echo; 'Stand by me' (p70) has a sung ostinato part; 'Swing low, sweet chariot' (p64) and 'El condor pasa' (p74) include canon sections and 'Cat and mouse games' (p66) features two partner songs.

Part-singing does not have to be a difficult, mysterious activity only performed by serious choirs, but is something that can be done by everyone in an enjoyable, fun way. 'Banana Splits' provides you with everything you need to make the first steps into part-singing easy and entertaining for 7-11 year olds. And it'll be fun for you too!

Banana splits
a simple chant with actions

Bananas, bananas, clap, clap, clap,
Bananas, bananas, flap, flap, flap.
Bananas, bananas, click, click, click,
Bananas, bananas, flick, flick, flick.
Bananas, bananas, bump, bump, bump,
Bananas, bananas, jump, jump, jump.

This chant can be performed with or without the piano accompaniment given.

Chant the words and perform the actions suggested by the words. When the chant is familiar leave out the action words and chant 'bananas, bananas', followed by the action only.

Divide the pupils into two groups. As one group performs the original chant, the other can chant this back-to-front version:

Clap, clap, clap; bananas, bananas,
Flap, flap, flap; bananas, bananas ...

Perform the two versions of the chants with actions. Try leaving out the action words.

Words and music by Ana Sanderson

8

Clap your hands an action song

1

Verse

Clap, clap, clap your hands,
Clap your hands together,
Clap, clap, clap your hands,
Clap your hands together.

Interlude 1  2

Tap, tap, tap your chin...

Interlude 1  2

Press, press, press your nose...

Interlude 1  2

Pat, pat, pat your head...

Interlude 1 2

Bang, bang, bang your fists...

Interlude 1 2

The pupils sing each verse without actions. The actions shown are performed with a partner during the interlude.

The one-handed actions are easier to perform if both partners use only right hands or only left hands.

Traditional North American
Actions contributed by Jane Sebba

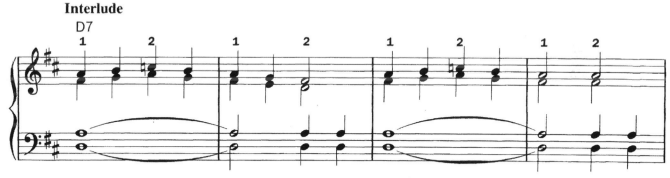

Choo choo

a song with a 'choo choo' chant

Once there was a choo choo,
But he couldn't choo choo,
So the story goes.
Instead of saying choo choo,
All he said was atchoo,
Because he had a cold in his nose.
A - a - a - tchoo!
    Choo, choo, choo ...

Words and music by Bob Schafer, Duke Ellington and Dave Ringler

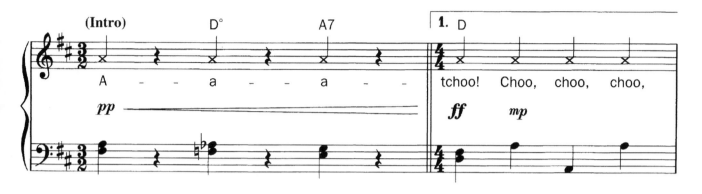

The children sing the song up to 'atchoo!' while gently walking in time with the pulse marked **x** in the music. (If space is confined, move arms like train pistons.) They then make a 'choo' sound like a train on each pulse. While everyone 'choos', play or hum the song melody.

Divide the pupils into two groups to sing 'Choo choo' as a two-part song:

1	verse	choos	verse	etc
2		verse	choos	etc

Repeat as often as you like. To end the performance, both groups stop on the '-tchoo' of 'a-tchoo!'.

Chuffers and sneezers a warm-up game

Play this game before singing 'Choo choo'. You will need a large space.

Whisper either 'chuffer' or 'sneezer' to each pupil in the class; alternatively, the pupils can secretly choose to be one or the other.

When the teacher says '1, 2, 3, go!', each pupil makes the sound of his or her word. The 'chuffers' make train sounds and the 'sneezers' make sneezing sounds. Everyone tries to find other 'chuffers' or 'sneezers' by listening to the sounds, in order to form two groups. The groups are then ready to begin singing a two-part song.

Nanuma (short version) a game for copying

1   Nanuma wyaeh, Nanuma. **x x x**
2   Nanuma wyaeh, Nanuma. **x x x**

Na – nu – ma wy – a – eh,   Na – nu – ma.

Sit in a circle. Teach the song as an echo song. Clap on each of the three beats marked 'x' at the end of the line. When the children are familiar with the song, begin the game.

Tuned percussion accompaniment

You or a chosen pupil leads. The leader sings the song and instead of clapping on the **x** beats, makes up something new for the others to copy, e.g. a pattern of body sounds, a different clapping pattern, or some new words. Everyone then sings and copies what the leader did.

Keep the new ideas simple. Keep the song going without breaks between repeats.

Here are some suggested improvisations to do on the three **x** beats:

Traffic lights   a game with signals

For this game, you (or a chosen leader) will need a set of three cards: a green card, a red card and an amber card.

Choose any song that everyone knows well, such as 'She'll be coming round the mountain' or 'My bonnie lies over the ocean'.

While the green card shows, everyone sings out loud. While the red card shows, everyone sings silently in their heads. When the green card shows again, everyone sings out loud.

Try it.

Did everyone sing the same word when the green card reappeared? If not, tap a drum in time to the music, ask the children to walk in time to the music, or show the red card for a shorter time.

When everyone is used to the red and green cards, introduce the amber card. While the amber card shows, everyone claps the rhythm of the words.

Divide the children into two groups and choose two leaders, each with a set of three cards. The leaders conduct their groups by starting with the green card, then showing the cards in any order. The groups may or may not be responding to the same colours at the same time, but should start the song together and keep in time with each other.

Contributed by Helen MacGregor

Jack-in-the-box a game with signals

You will need four conductor's cards for this game. You can use enlarged photocopies of the pictures opposite or make your own.

Introduce the cards one at a time and explain each instruction. Then ask everyone to sing a well-known action song, such as 'Heads, shoulders, knees and toes'. Show the cards in any order to the pupils as they perform the song. The pupils should follow the card instructions as they perform.

When everyone is familiar with the game, try showing pairs of cards where both activities can be done at once. Clapping and performing the actions or singing in your head and singing out loud are not possible to do at the same time!

Choose four pupils to be the 'jack-in-the-boxes'. Each holds one of the cards. They sit in a row on chairs facing the other pupils. The teacher stands facing the jack-in-the-boxes but behind the other pupils. The jack-in-the-boxes watch the teacher very carefully for signals to stand up and sit down. When a jack-in-the-box stands, the children must do as the card instructs. If two jack-in-the-boxes stand at once, the children must perform the activities on both cards.

Photocopiable material

Contributed by Helen MacGregor and Jane Sebba

Sing out loud

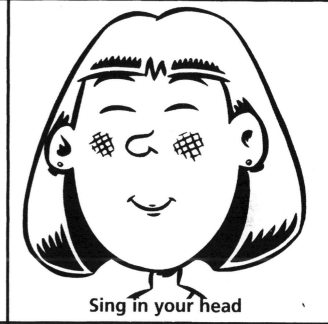
Sing in your head

Do the actions

Clap the rhythm of the words

Mister Clicketty Cane
a cumulative song with echoes in the verse

1+2 Chorus
When Mister Clicketty Cane
Plays his silly game,
All the kids in the street,
They like to do the same.

Verse 1
1 Wash your face in orange juice,
2 Wash your face in orange juice.

Chorus

Verse 2
1 Clean your teeth with bubble gum,
2 Clean your teeth with bubble gum,
1 Wash your face in orange juice,
2 Wash your face in orange juice.

Chorus

Verse 3
1 Fix the fence with sticky tape,
2 Fix the fence with sticky tape,
1 Clean your teeth with bubble gum,
2 Clean your teeth with bubble gum,
1 Wash your face in orange juice,
2 Wash your face in orange juice.

Chorus

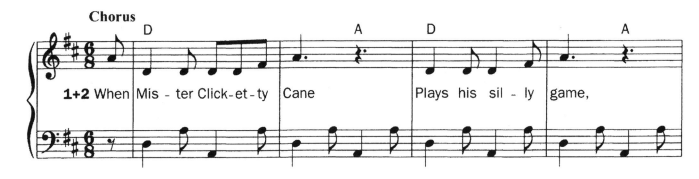

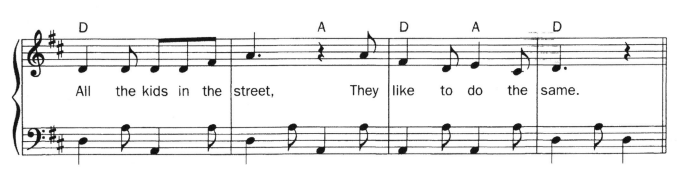

Verses 1-6 (repeat as necessary)

D.C. (except after verse 6)

Final chorus

1+2 When Mis-ter Click-et-ty Cane | Plays his sil – ly game, | All the kids in the

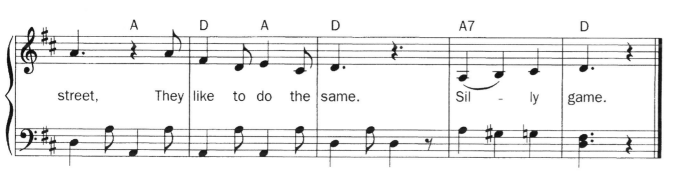

street, They like to do the same. Sil – ly game.

Verse 4

1 Brush your hair with a toothbrush,
2 Brush your hair with a toothbrush,
1 Fix the fence with sticky tape,
2 Fix the fence with sticky tape ...
(continue with all verses)

Chorus

Verse 5

1 Fry an egg on a slippery dip,
2 Fry an egg on a slippery dip,
1 Brush your hair with a toothbrush,
2 Brush your hair with a
      toothbrush ...
(continue with all verses)

Chorus

Verse 6

1 Belly flop in a pizza,
2 Belly flop in a pizza,
1 Fry an egg on a slippery dip,
2 Fry an egg on a slippery dip ...
(continue with all verses)

Final chorus
...Silly game!

Words and music by Peter Combe

Sing a little song
an echo song

1+2 Sing a little song
      of sunny skies.
1 Sing a little song,
2 Sing a little song.
1+2 Run and catch the sunlight
      in your eyes.
1 Sing a little song,
2 Sing a little song.
1+2 And we all will smile,
      for nothing can go wrong,
1 When we sing a little song,
2 Sing a little song,
1 Sing a little song,
2 Sing a little song.

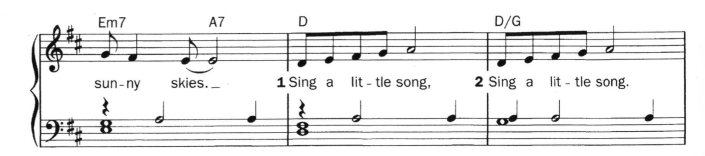

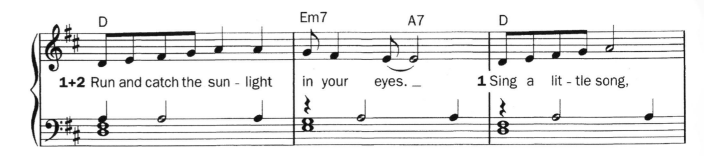

Words and music by Henry E Dennis, Junior

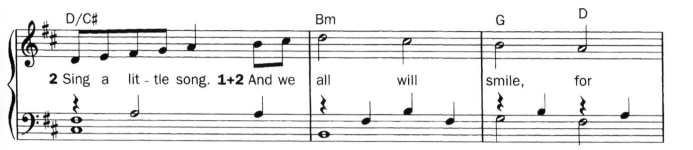

2 Sing a lit-tle song. **1+2** And we all will smile, for

no-thing can go wrong, **1** When we sing a lit-tle song, **2** Sing a lit-tle

When everyone is familiar with the song, group 1 can try holding on the last note of each 'sing a little song' phrase, while group 2 sings the echo.

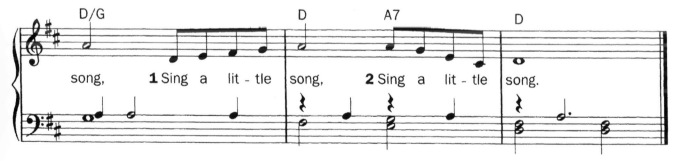

song, **1** Sing a lit-tle song, **2** Sing a lit-tle song.

Ewe! a call and response song

1   O ma sifun inkululeko,
2   Ewe!
1   Masiye pambile mntwana,
2   Ewe!

Tuned percussion accompaniment

Untuned percussion accompaniment

Translation
Oh mother, we want peace,
Yes!
Let's move forwards child,
Yes!

Pronunciation
Oh mah see-foon in-koo-loo-le-ko.
Eh-weh!
Ma-see-yeh pam-bee-leh moont-wah-nah.
Eh-weh!

Either divide the pupils into two groups, or
choose a soloist to sing the call (part 1).

*Xhosa words by Sue Lubner and Tamar Swade
Music by Tamar Swade*

1 O ma si - fun in - ku - lu - le - ko, __ 2 E - we!

1 Ma - si - ye pam - bi - le mnt - wa - na, 2 E - we! *(spoken)*

1 Ma __ si - fun in - ku - lu - le - ko, __ 2 E - we!

1 Ma - si - ye pam - bi - le mnt - wa - na, 2 E - we! *(spoken)*

Which note? a call and response game

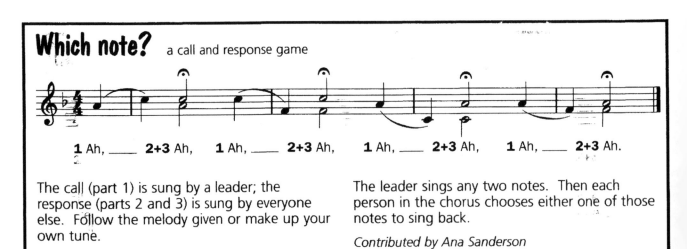

1 Ah, ___ 2+3 Ah,   1 Ah, ___ 2+3 Ah,   1 Ah, ___ 2+3 Ah,   1 Ah, ___ 2+3 Ah.

The call (part 1) is sung by a leader; the
response (parts 2 and 3) is sung by everyone
else. Follow the melody given or make up your
own tune.

The leader sings any two notes. Then each
person in the chorus chooses either one of those
notes to sing back.

Contributed by Ana Sanderson

The green cross code

a call and response song

1 Always use the green cross code,
2 When you're crossing the road,
   my friend.
1 Look right, look left, look right
   down the road,
2 When you're crossing the road,
   my friend.
1 If the road is clear you're ready
   to go,
2 When you're crossing the road,
   my friend.
1 Walk over quick, but don't run
   or be slow,
2 When you're crossing the road,
   my friend.

Tuned percussion accompaniment

Divide the pupils into two groups. The groups
stand in two lines facing each other across a
room. Everyone sings the song; on the last line
of the song, both groups can cross the room.

Words and music by Ana Sanderson

19

Have you ever?

a question and answer song with actions

1 Have you ever, ever, ever, in your
   long-legged life,
   Seen a long-legged sailor with a
   long-legged wife?
2 No, I've never, ever, ever, in my
   long-legged life,
   Seen a long-legged sailor with a
   long-legged wife.

1 Have you ever, ever, ever, in your
   short-legged life …
2 No, I've never, ever, ever, in my
   short-legged life …

1 Have you ever, ever, ever, in your
   one-legged life …
2 No, I've never, ever, ever in my
   one-legged life …

Follow the symbols in the music to perform the
clapping pattern:

k	tap knees
h	clap hands
a	action -
	'long' - hands far apart
	'short' - hands close together
	'one' - hold up one finger

Traditional

20

The telephone song

1 Hey Helen.
2 I hear you calling my name.
1 Hey Helen.
2 I hear you calling again.
1 There's someone on the telephone.
2 If that is Richard then I'm not
    at home.
All With a rick *click* tick ticketty tick,
    oh yeah!
    With a rick *click* tick ticketty tick.

On *click*, click your fingers.

Tuned percussion accompaniment

Traditional American

Sit in a circle. Choose a leader to begin.

First time:
The first person (singing part 1) phones a second person (singing part 2), who names a third person.

Second time
The second person (now singing part 1) phones the third person (now singing part 2), who names a fourth person.

Third time
The third person (now singing part 1) phones the fourth person (now singing part 2), who names a fifth person.

Sing the song as many times as you like. Everyone can join in with the last two lines. Names should be sung so that they fit into the song without losing the feel of the beat throughout.

Poppycock pie
a conversation rap

1 Can you do what I do?
Will you have a try?
Can you paddle on a poodle,
With a pickle in your eye?

2 No, I can't do that,
And I'll tell you why,
I'm too busy eating
Poppycock pie!

1+2 Chorus
Pop, pop,
Pop, pop, pop, pop,
Pop, pop, poppycock,
Poppycock pie!

1 Can you do what I do?
Will you have a try?
Can you tango with a turnip,
When the moon is in the sky?

2 No, I can't do that,
And I'll tell you why,
I'm too busy eating
Poppycock pie!

1+2 Chorus
Pop, pop …

1 Can you do what I do?
Will you have a try?
Can you wrestle with a rhino,
In a big bow tie?

2 No, I can't do that …

1+2 Chorus
Pop, pop,
Pop, pop, pop, pop,
What a load-a poppycock,
Poppycock pie!

Kaye Umansky

Form two groups to perform the rap as written.

Alternatively, accompany the rap by chanting the 'pop, pop' chorus throughout. You can form a third group to do this, or group 2 can chant the chorus during group 1's verse and vice versa.

Time for a 'hocket' a singing game

'Hocketting' can be done by two groups of pupils or two individuals.

Choose a well-known tune, such as 'Kum ba yah', Twinkle, twinkle, little star', 'Doe a deer' or 'Supercalifragilistic'. Group 1 sings the first note, group 2 sings the second note, group 1 the third, group 2 the fourth, and so on.

If a note pitch is repeated in the melody, the melody stays with the same group.

'Kumbayah' would begin like this:

1	2
Kum	ba
yah, my Lord,	Kum ba
yah,	Kum
ba	yah, my Lord,
Kum	ba
yah ...	

Contributed by Helen MacGregor

I hear the bells
a conversation song

1   I hear the bells go
       ding, ding, ding,

2   I hear the bells go
       dong, dong, dong,

1   I go ding,

2   I go dong,

1+2 All day long.

1	**2**
Ding,	dong, dong,
ding, ding,	dong, dong,
ding, ding,	dong, dong,
ding.	

1   I hear the drums go
       bang, bang, bang,

2   I hear the drums go
       boom, boom, boom ...

1   I hear my hands go
       clap, clap, clap,

2   I hear my hands go
       tap, tap, tap ...

Words and music by David Moses

At a moderate tempo

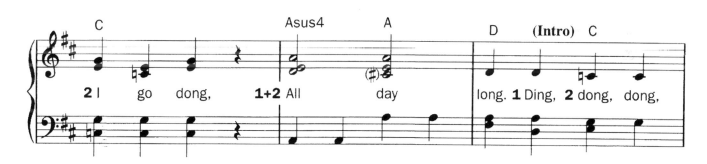

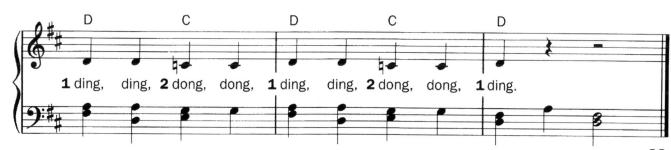

Dham dham dham *an echo song*

1 Dham, dham, dham, dham,
   dhamaru bhaje,

2 Dham, dham, dham, dham,
   dhamaru bhaje.

1 Hara bola nata shiva shambo bhaje,

2 Hara bola nata shiva shambo bhaje.

1 Ghana, ghana, ghana, ghana,
   ghanta bhaje,

2 Ghana, ghana, ghana, ghana,
   ghanta bhaje,

1 Hara bola nata shiva shambo bhaje,

2 Hara bola nata shiva shambo bhaje.

Translation
The drum beats, to sing in praise of Lord Shiva,
Sing in praise of the spiritual father, Lord Shiva,
The bells ring, to sing in praise of Lord Shiva,
Sing in praise of the spiritual father, Lord Shiva.

Pronunciation
Dam, dam, dam, dam, dam-ah-roo bah-jeh ...
Hah-rah boh-lah nah-tah shee-vah
   jam-boh bah-jeh ...
Gan-ah, gan-ah, gan-ah, gan-ah,
   gan-tah bah-jeh ...

Tuned percussion accompaniment

Traditional Hindu

24

Tongo

an echo song

1 Tongo,
2 Tongo,
1 Tongo,
2 Tongo.
1 Chimné bahé, bahé, oh,
2 Chimné bahé, bahé, oh,
1 Chimné bahé, bahé, oh,
2 Chimné bahé, bahé, oh.
1 Oo away,
2 Oo away,
1 Oo away,
2 Oo away.
1 Balay kalow away.
2 Balay kalow away.

Tuned percussion accompaniment

F   F   F   F

'Tongo' is a Polynesian canoeing song.

Hold on to the last note of every phrase while the other group sings its next phrase.

Traditional Polynesian

TV tantrum a conversation chant

1 Turn the TV off and go to bed now,
2 Oh no I won't!
1 Turn the TV off and go to bed now,
2 Oh no I won't!

1
Turn it off,
Go to bed,

2
Everytime I want to
watch a programme that
I really like, it's 'No!'

1 If you get no sleep you will turn
  yellow.
2 Oh no I won't!

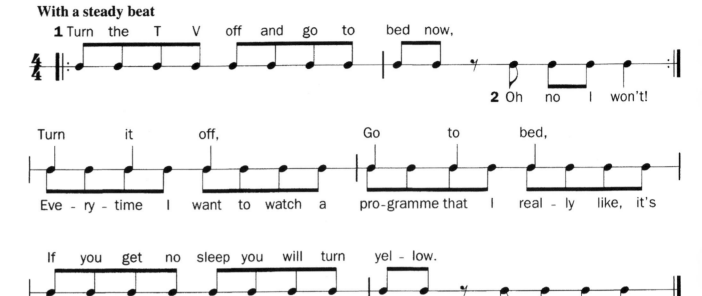

Chant the words rhythmically. Play a steady drum beat with the chant to help keep time.

Teach the beginning and end of the chant first. The middle part is quite tricky; practise it separately, then fit it into the chant.

Develop your performance further by clapping or tapping the rhythm of the words instead of chanting.

Diana Thompson

Tambourine talk a conversation game with instruments

Each pupil needs a partner and an untuned percussion instrument.

Begin by introducing words, such as 'happy', 'secretive', 'lively', or 'noisy', that can describe conversations. Each pair of pupils chooses a word, and using the instruments only, performs a 'conversation' in the style of that word while everyone else listens. When the conversation is finished, everyone else suggests words that might describe it.

Put the percussion instruments away. Ask the pupils to converse with each other using vocal sounds only but no real words! Continue using words to describe the conversations.

Contributed by Helen MacGregor

Sports day race a conversation chant

1
Get ready!
Are you ready?
Get
Get
And

Don't wait,
Or be late,
Get

It's speed,
That you need,
Get
Get
And

1+2   Go! Go! Go!

2
Get ready!
I'm ready!
ready,
steady,
go!

Get ready!
I'm ready!
ready ...

Get ready!
I'm ready!
ready,
steady,

Ana Sanderson

Fast, with a steady beat

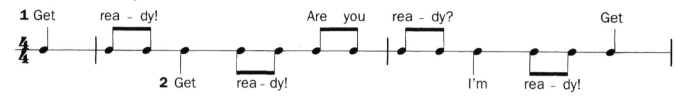

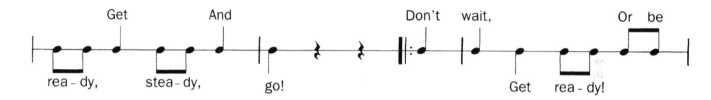

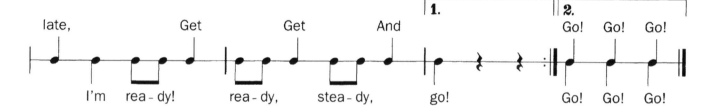

Jungle sounds a game chant for inventing sounds

Sit in a circle to perform this chant:

I was walking in the jungle
And heard a strange sound.
(Count to four silently)

During the four counts, a member of the group improvises a sound effect using vocal or body sounds. Everyone performs the chant again and the next person in the circle performs a different sound effect. This process is repeated over and over again. No sound effect can be copied or performed twice.

See how many different sounds everyone can make up before someone runs out of new ideas.

Contributed by Helen MacGregor

Down by the bay
an echo song

1	Down by the bay,
2	Down by the bay,
1	Where the watermelons grow,
2	Where the watermelons grow,
1	Back to my home,
2	Back to my home,
1	I dare not go,
2	I dare not go.
1	For if I do,
2	For if I do,
1	My mother will say,
2	My mother will say,
1+2	'Did you ever see a cow,
	With a green eyebrow,
1	Down by the bay?'
2	Down by the bay.

Traditional English

Either divide the pupils into two groups to sing this song or choose a leader to sing part 1. Invent new, funny words for what the mother says.

More jungle sounds — a game for improvising layered sound effects

Sit in a circle to perform this chant:

**I was walking in the jungle,
And heard a strange sound.**
*(Count to four silently and
repeat as necessary)*

During the four counts, someone makes a sound effect. The chant is then repeated.

The next person in the circle makes a different sound effect; then both sound effects are performed at the same time.

The chant is repeated and a third person makes a new sound. All three sound effects are then performed simultaneously.

Continue until everyone in the circle has joined in with a sound effect.

Contributed by Helen MacGregor

Make up your own ostinato (1) — a rhythmic ostinato activity

Divide the pupils into small groups. Give each group an empty grid based on the one shown. The grid can be used in various ways for notating ideas for rhythmic ostinatos (rhythmic patterns repeated over and over again). The columns indicate beats 1, 2, 3 and 4. The rows can indicate body percussion sounds, percussion instruments, and members of the group. Each row can be read on its own, or any (or all) of the rows can be read simultaneously. Repeat the lines over and over again to make an ostinato.

The example grid opposite shows how a grid might be used.

Each group decides which sound effects should be included in its rhythmic ostinato, who should perform them, and on which of the four beats. They use the grid to notate their rhythmic ostinato.

Groups may like to try out their ideas with performances of 'Four white horses' (p31) or 'Nanuma' (p34).

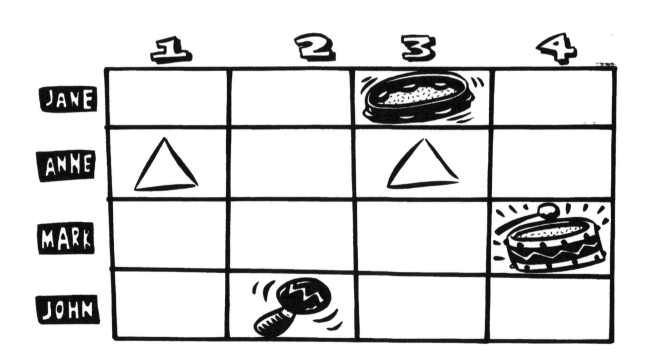

Four white horses
a song with a clapping pattern

Four white horses on the river,
Hey, hey, hey, up tomorrow,
Up tomorrow is a rainy day,
Come on and join our shadow play.
Shadow play is a ripe banana,
Up tomorrow is a rainy day.

Each pupil needs a partner to do the accompanying clapping pattern.

1   Clap right hands together
2   Clap own hands
3   Clap left hands together
4   Clap own hands
5   Clap both hands of partner
6   Clap own hands

Try the clapping pattern at the same time as singing the song. Alternatively, the pupils can make up their own ostinato pattern to play along with the song. (See 'Make up your own ostinato (1)' on p30.)

An optional descant harmony line is shown in small notes.

Traditional, Virgin Islands

31

Parade day! an ostinato chant

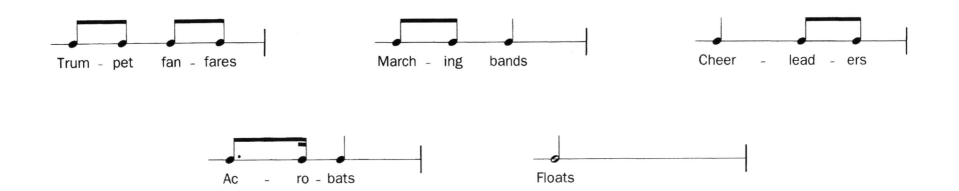

Begin by familiarising everyone with each chant.

The pupils then sit in two rows of equal length, facing each other. The first facing pair of children are appointed leaders.

The teacher chooses two of the chants and allocates one to each leader. While lightly tapping a marching beat which continues throughout, the teacher counts 1 2 3 4 to signal to the row leaders to begin. Each row leader chants his or her

words, followed in turn by each person in the row. Everyone must try to chant at the right moment and in time with the drum beat.

Contributed by Ana Sanderson

Beat box a game for making up layers of sound

Sit in a circle.

The teacher or a leader begins singing a short musical phrase over and over again, e.g. do, do, do, do-bee, do, do, do-oo (all on one note). The next person in the circle improvises a short melody or vocal effect to go with the leader's line, e.g. lah-, lah-, lah-, lah-.

The next person improvises something different, and so on, each person adding a new layer of sound.

When you have finished, discuss the end effect. Was it good? Too complex? Was anyone too loud? Do you need a finishing sign?

Try the game again. Can you improve on your first go?

Contributed by Helen MacGregor

The shark a chant with a spoken ostinato

3

2 Ostinato part
Doo-doo, doo bedee doo,
Doo-doo, doo bedee doo,

1 Story part
   There was a boy,
2 Doo-doo, doo bedee doo,
1   There was a girl,
2 Doo-doo, doo bedee doo,
1   They went for a swim,
2 Doo-doo …
1   A swim in the sea.
2 Doo-doo …
1   They took off their clothes,
2 Doo-doo …
1   All of their clothes,
2 Doo-doo …
1   They swam so far,
2 Doo-doo …
1   Really far.
2 Doo-doo …
1   There was no one around,
2 Doo-doo …
1   Just no one around,
2 Doo-doo …
1   Totally empty,
2 Doo-doo …
1   Except for the sharks!
2 Na-na, na na na na!

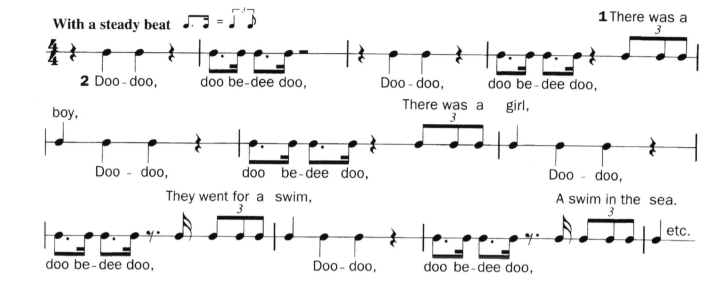

With a steady beat

1   Daddy shark,
2 Na-na, na na na na!
1   Mummy shark,
2 Ma-ma, ma ma ma ma!
1   Granpa shark,
2 Ma-ma, ma ma ma ma!
1   Baby shark,
2 Wee-wee, wee wee wee wee!
1   They swam so fast
2 Doo-doo, doo bedee doo,
1   Really fast,
2 Doo-doo …
1   To the shore,
2 Doo-doo …
1   Out of the water,
2 Doo-doo …

1   Ran so fast,
2 Doo-doo …
1   Really fast,
2 Doo-doo …
1   Totally empty,
2 Doo-doo …
1   No habitation,
2 Doo-doo …
1   Except for the sharks!

Group 1 chants the story as group 2 chants the ostinato. Encourage group 2 to keep the chant going steadily.

Individuals can devise their own stories to chant as everyone else performs the ostinato.

Traditional; collected by Nancy Kerr

Nanuma (extended version)
a song with a sung ostinato

Nanuma wyaeh, Nanuma.
Nanuma wyaeh, Nanuma.
Nanuma wyaeh, Nanuma.
Nanuma wyaeh, Nanuma.

Moderately

Na - nu - ma wy - a - eh, Na - nu - ma. Na -

- nu - ma wy - a - eh, Na - nu - ma. Na - nu - ma wy - a - eh, Na -

- nu - ma. Na - nu - ma wy - a - eh, Na - nu - ma.

Tuned percussion accompaniment

D E D D

Sung ostinato

Na - nu - ma wy - a - eh, Na - nu - ma.

You can devise a rhythmic ostinato to perform with 'Nanuma' (see 'Make up your own ostinato (1)' on p30).

'Nanuma' can also be performed with the sung ostinato shown above. It can also be performed as a round; the round entry points are marked *.

Traditional African

Make up your own ostinato (2) a pitched ostinato activity

Use chime bars tuned to C D F G A. Have at least two sets available for each group.

Divide the pupils into small groups. Each group can devise a short ostinato using any or all of these five notes. Encourage the groups to sing and play their ostinatos. Empty grids based on the one opposite may be used for notating the ostinatos.

Groups members can take it in turns to improvise melodies using the five notes, while other group members perform the ostinato.

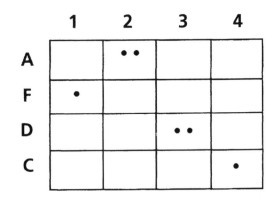

	1	2	3	4
A		••		
F	•			
D			••	
C				•

I love the flowers

a song with a sung ostinato

2 Ostinato part

Boom de boom do do do,

Boom de boom do do do...

1 I love the flowers,
   I love the daffodils,
   I love the mountains,
   I love the rolling hills.
   I love the fireside,
   When all the lights are low.
   Boom-de-ah-ra, boom-de-ah-ra,
      boom-de-ah-ra, boom!

Tuned percussion accompaniment

Divide the pupils into two groups to perform this song with the ostinato.

End the song by repeating the last line of the music (and ostinato) over and over again, gradually getting quieter and quieter until the sound dies away to nothing.

'I love the flowers' can be sung as a two, three or four part round. The entry points are marked * in the music. The ostinato part can be sung with the round.

Traditional

35

How doth the little crocodile
a song with a sung ostinato

2 Ostinato part
Dm dm, dm dm, dm ba-dm, ba-dm ba,
Dm dm, dm dm, dm ba-dm, ba-dm ba,
Dm dm, dm dm, dm dm, dm dm,
Dm, *(Whisper)* two, three, four,
(Sing) dm ba-dm, dm dm ...

1 How doth the little crocodile,
Improve his shining tail, his tail,
And pour the waters of the Nile,
On ev'ry golden, ev'ry golden,
golden scale!

How cheerfully he seems to grin,
How neatly spreads his claws,
his claws,
And welcomes little fishes in,
With gently smiling, gently smiling,
smiling jaws!

How doth the little crocodile ...

On ev'ry golden, ev'ry golden,
golden scale!?

Words (slightly adapted) by Lewis Carroll
Music by Malcolm Abbs

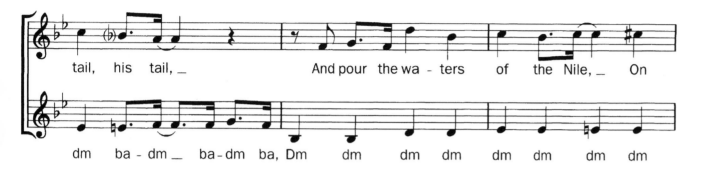

tail, his tail, _ And pour the wa - ters of the Nile, _ On

dm ba - dm _ ba - dm ba, Dm dm dm dm dm dm dm dm

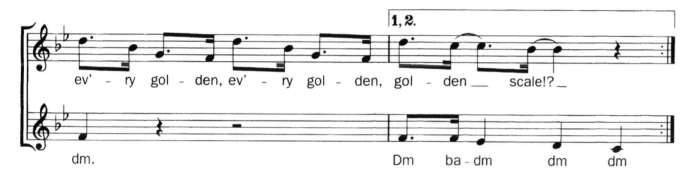

1, 2.

ev' - ry gol - den, ev' - ry gol - den, gol - den _ scale!? _

dm. Dm ba - dm dm dm

3.

gol - den _ scale. _ On ev' - ry gol - den, ev' - ry gol - den, gol - den _ scale!? _

Dm ba - dm dm _ dm Dm ba - dm dm _ dm.

Pretend you are imitating a double bass being plucked in jazz style when you sing the ostinato part.

The pupils in group 2 can click their fingers on the second and fourth crotchet beats to add to the swing feel.

The band
a song with several ostinatos

1 Verses

I hear the band far away,
far away, far away.
I hear the band far away,
far away, far away.

I hear the band near the town ...

I hear the band marching by ...

I hear the band leave the town ...

I hear the band far away ...

2 1st ostinato (all verses)

Drum drum drum drum ...

3 2nd ostinato (verses 2, 3 and 4)

Bom bom bom bom ...

4 3rd ostinato (verse 3 only)

Tootle tootle tootle tootle toot ...

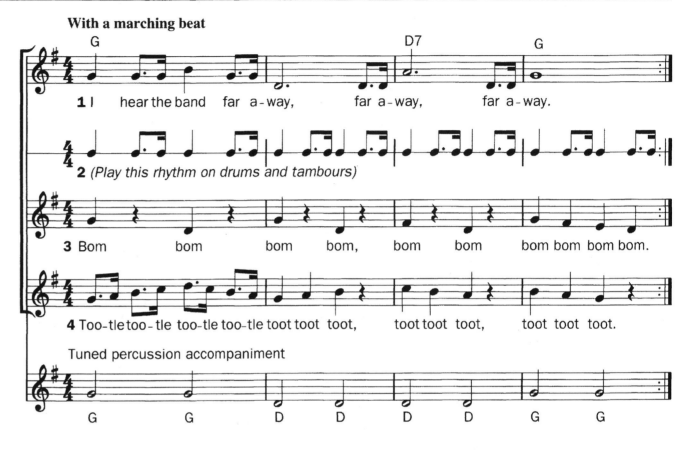

With a marching beat

1 I hear the band far a-way, far a-way, far a-way.

2 *(Play this rhythm on drums and tambours)*

3 Bom bom bom bom, bom bom bom bom bom bom.

4 Too-tle too-tle too-tle too-tle toot toot toot, toot toot toot, toot toot toot.

Tuned percussion accompaniment

This song begins very quietly when the band is far away, gradually gets louder as the band gets nearer, and fades as the band goes away.

There are three ostinato parts to be performed with this song - a 'drum' part, a 'tuba' part and a 'trumpet' part.

To perform the whole song, divide the pupils into four groups - one big group which sings the verses, and three smaller groups which perform the ostinatos.

Group 2 performs all five verses, starting quietly, getting louder, then quieter. Group 3 performs during verses 2, 3 and 4 only. Group 4 performs during verse 3 only.

The tuned percussion accompaniment given is optional.

Words and music by Sue Nicholls

Can you dig that crazy gibberish?

a chanted round

Chorus

Can you dig that crazy gibberish?
Can you dig it? Can you dig it?
Can you dig that crazy gibberish?
Can you dig it? Can you dig it?

Verse

Oh look, there's a chicken coming
    down the road,
Oh look, there's another one sitting
    on the fence.
Maa, maa,
'Get that whatsamagig off my tractor!'

This round can be performed in two, three or four parts. The entry points are marked * in the music. Repeat the chant as often as you wish, beginning and ending with the chorus.

Make sure that the words are chanted rhythmically. Mark the pulse by clapping or marching as you chant the words.

Traditional

39

Autumn leaves
a canon

4

Autumn leaves are falling,
Orange, red and brown,
See them twirling in the wind,
And floating to the ground.

Tuned percussion accompaniment

C B A G F E D C

Anonymous

Gently

Au - tumn leaves are fall - ing, O - range, red and brown.

See them swirl - ing in the wind, And float - ing to the ground.

The canon entry point is marked * in the music.

Music alone shall live
a canon

All things shall perish from
        under the sky.
Music alone shall live,
        music alone shall live,
Music alone shall live, never to die.

Tuned percussion accompaniment

F   G   C   F

Traditional German

With dignity

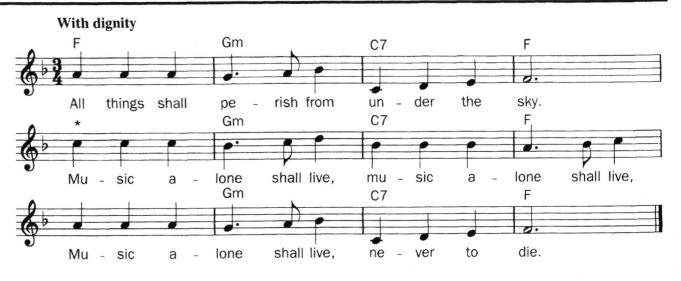

All things shall pe - rish from un - der the sky.

Mu - sic a - lone shall live, mu - sic a - lone shall live,

Mu - sic a - lone shall live, ne - ver to die.

The canon entry point is marked * in the music.

40

Kum bachur atzel a round

Kum bachur atzel, ve tse la-avodah,
Kum bachur atzel, ve tse la-avodah,
Kum, kum, ve tse la-avodah,
Kum, kum, ve tse la-avodah,
Kukuriku, kukuriku, tarnegol karah,
Kukuriku, kukuriku, tarnegol karah.

The round entry points are marked * in the music.

Translation
Get up, lazy boy, and go to work.
The cock is crowing.

Pronunciation
Koom bak-chur (ch as in loch) ah-tzell,
Veh-tseh lah-ah-voh-dah,
Koo-koo-ree-koo ... tah-neh-gol kah-rah.

Tuned percussion accompaniment

Moderately

Kum ba-chur at-zel, __ ve tse la-a-vo-dah, Kum ba-chur at-zel, __ ve tse la-a-vo-dah.

Kum, _____ kum, __ ve tse la-a-vo-dah, Kum, _____ kum, __ ve tse la-a-vo-dah.

Ku-ku-ri-ku, ku-ku-ri-ku, tar-ne-gol ka-rah, Ku-ku-ri-ku, ku-ku-ri-ku, tar-ne-gol ka-rah.

Traditional Israeli

Behind the action a game in the form of a round

'Behind the action' helps develop the ability to perform one action while observing another action to be copied later.

Everyone counts eight beats out loud as you perform a simple action, such as clapping on the beat. Everyone observes your action, then performs it during the next eight counts. As the pupils perform the first action, you perform a new, second action. After eight more counts, the pupils change to the second action, as you change to a third action. Continue for as long as you wish.

Before you play the game, make sure everyone

is familiar with the rules. If possible, everyone should stand up to play.

You can make 'Behind the action' harder by –

* making the actions more difficult

* counting silently

* reducing the number of counts

* dividing the pupils into two (or more) groups, so that group 1 copies the teacher, group 2 copies group 1, and so on.

Contributed by Ana Sanderson

Emanuel
a canon with actions

Verse 1

One Monday morn,
The king, his wife and son, Emanuel,
Came to me at home,
To hear the latest scandal.
After they'd been fed,
The young Emanuel said,
'Since there's so much to say,
We'll come another day.'

Verse 2

Friday at five ...

Verse 3

Sunday at six ...
After they'd been fed,
The young Emanuel said,
'I've got an awful head,
Let's all go home to bed.'

The canon entry point is marked * in the music.

Traditional French melody
Words translated by Peter Honniball

(Intro)   A7

said, 'Since there's so much to say, We'll come a - no - ther

1, 2.   3.
D   D

day.'   bed.'

Divide the pupils into two groups and follow this performance plan:

Verse 1 - both groups sing together
Verse 2 - both groups sing and perform the actions suggested below
Verse 3 - the two groups sing the canon while performing the actions.

Perform these actions during verses 2 and 3:

'the king'	hold a hand up high to show a tall man
'his wife'	hold your hand slightly lower to show a shorter woman
'and son, Emanuel'	hold one hand low down to show a short boy
'came to'	do a beckoning action
'me'	point to yourself
'at home'	make a roof, holding your fingertips together
'to hear'	cup your right hand around your right ear
'latest scandal'	make a stirring action with your hands
'fed'	mime eating
'say'	waggle your index finger
'head' (verse 3)	hold your head with both hands
'go home to bed'	place your hands together and rest your head on them

Jelly on a plate

a four part round

Jel - ly on a plate, jel - ly on a plate, Wib - ble wob - ble, wib - ble wob - ble, Jel - ly on a plate.

Bis - cuits in the tin, bis - cuits in the tin, Throw them up, throw them up, Bis - cuits in the tin.

Fire on the floor, fire ___ on the floor, Stamp it out, stamp it out, Fire on the floor.

Can - dles on the cake, can - dles on the cake, Blow them out, blow them out, Fwh, fwh, fwh.

Jelly on a plate, jelly on a plate,
Wibble, wobble, wibble, wobble,
Jelly on a plate.

Biscuits in the tin, biscuits in the tin,
Throw them up, throw them up,
Biscuits in the tin.

Fire on the floor, fire on the floor,
Stamp it out, stamp it out,
Fire on the floor.

Candles on the cake, candles on the cake,
Blow them out, blow them out,
Fwh, fwh, fwh.

Tuned percussion accompaniment

D   D   D   D

The round entry points are marked * in the music.

Traditional words
Music by Tamar Swade

44

The human drum kit

Are you ready?
  'Cause you're in for a treat,
Are you ready with your
  fingers and feet,
Are you ready?
  Can you feel the beat?
We are the human drum kit!

Chorus (round)

Stamp, stamp!
  goes the big bass drum,
Now listen to the hi-hat,
  ch ch, ch ch,
Snares go
  clap clap, clap clap,
Followed by a crash on the cymbals,
  sh.

Perform the whole chant together. Then perform the chorus as a round in two, three or four parts. The round entry points are marked * in the music.

Try the chorus as a round with sound effects only; say the words silently in your head.

Ana Sanderson

45

Tomorrow's another day
a canon

Ooh lullah lay,
Another evening fades away,
I know the golden sun won't
        disappear for long,
Because tomorrow's another day.
(And I say ...)

Tuned percussion accompaniment

Words and music by Ana Sanderson

The canon entry point is marked * in the music.

Fiddle diddle
a canon

A-hum, fiddle diddle,
        a-hum, fiddle diddle,
A-hum, fiddle diddle,
        a-hum, fiddle diddle,
Oh can you do the tango,
The waltz, or the fandango?

A-hum, fiddle diddle ...
I cannot do the tango,
The waltz, or the fandango!

Words and music by Ana Sanderson

The canon entry point is marked * in the music.

Food feast a game in canon form

'Food feast' helps develop one's ability to perform and listen at the same time.

Familiarise everyone with the short musical phrases associated with each picture. If you would like to chant the 'foods' rather than sing them, chant the rhythm given in the music.

Divide the pupils into two groups - the leaders and the copiers. You (or a chosen pupil) hold the signs so that only the leaders can see them. You can make signs out of cut up enlarged photocopies of the pictures opposite.

The leaders sing or chant the short phrase that is associated with the first sign. When the teacher calls 'now' or claps, the copiers join in. When the second sign is shown, the leaders sing the second musical phrase that goes with it. The copiers, however, must continue with the first phrase, while listening to the phrase sung by the leaders. When the teacher claps, they begin singing the new musical phrase.

Photocopiable material

Contributed by Ana Sanderson

pick - led plums and par - snips

ripe ba - na - nas

cau - li - flower cheese

baked po - ta - to pie

string - y spa - ghet - ti

ice - cream and jam

Rings and circles
a canon

Rings and circles circle round,
Circle round, circle round.
Drops of water never bound,
Circle round forever.
Rings and circles circle round,
Circle round, circle round,
Love that grows without a sound,
Circle round forever.

Words and music by Jan Harmon

The canon entry point is marked * in the music.

By the waters of Babylon
a three part round

By the waters, the waters of Babylon.
We sat down and wept, and wept
    for thee, Zion.
We remember thee, remember thee,
    remember thee, Zion.

Tuned percussion accompaniment

The round entry points are marked * in the music.

Traditional

48

Noah's shanty
a song with a chorus canon

1 Elephants and flamingos,
Kittiwakes and wild dingos,
Hornets and things with stingos,
Comin' up two by two.

1, then 2 Chorus
Here they come up the gang plank,
Here they come up the gang plank,
Here they come up the gang plank,
Comin' up two by two.

2 Caribou and dalmatians,
Rabbits and their relations,
On the boat sides crustaceans,
Comin' up two by two.

2, then 1 Chorus

1 Mocking birds mock anteaters,
Millipedes walk with cheetahs,
Beetles lead all six-feetahs,
Comin' up two by two.

1, then 2 Chorus

2 Hummingbirds start a sing-song,
Wombats have games of ping-pong,
Little chimps think they're King Kong,
Comin' up two by two.

2, then 1 Chorus

With a strong beat ♩ = c 76

E - le-phants and _____ fla - min - gos, Kit - ti - wakes and _____ wild din - gos,

Hor - nets and things _____ with stin - gos, Com-in' up two by two.

Chorus

Here they come up _____ the gang plank, Here they come up _____ the gang plank,

1. – 3.
Here they come up _____ the gang plank, Com-in' up two by two.

4.
Com in' up two by two, Com-in' up two by two.

Tuned percussion accompaniment

E   E   E   E
A   A   A   A

Clap hands on the first and third beats throughout the whole song. There are two possible entry points for the second group performing the chorus canon; these are at the bar * and at the half bar (*).

Words and music by Malcolm Abbs

Big Ben Bean an activity with a chant

1 Hi there, kids!
I'm Big Ben Bean,
And this thing here,
Is my joke machine.

2 A joke machine?
What can he mean?
Tell us all about it,
Big Ben Bean!

1 If you're feeling down,
If you're feeling blue,
My joke machine,
Is the thing for you.

1+2 Just give a little twiddle,
Give a little poke,
Stick your finger in the dial,
And out comes a joke.

Pause here for a child to tell a joke (e.g. "Ring, ring! Is that the lunatic asylum? Yes, but we're not on the 'phone!")

To keep the momentum of the rap going, quietly tap a drum beat throughout the joke.

After the joke, the two groups perform the choruses below at the same time.

1 Chorus
Joke Machine,
Joke Machine,
Big Ben Bean and his
Joke Machine.
Joke Machine,
Joke Machine,
Big Ben Bean and his
Joke Machine.

2 Chorus
That made me laugh,
That made me grin,
That made me giggle,
'Til my tummy caved in,
It's the best machine,
I ever have seen,
Let's hear another one,
Big Ben Bean.

Pause for another joke then repeat the chorus. Repeat this as many times as required. When everyone has told a joke, chant the final choruses below.

1 Final chorus
Joke Machine,
Joke Machine,
Big Ben Bean and his
Joke Machine.
Joke Machine,
Joke Machine,
Big Ben Bean and his
Joke Machine.

2 Final chorus
That made me laugh,
That made me grin,
That made me giggle,
'Til my tummy caved in.
It's the best machine,
I ever have seen,
No time for another one,
Big Ben Bean.

Kaye Umansky

London Bridge/Pease pudding hot partner songs

London Bridge is falling down,
Falling down, falling down,
London Bridge is falling down,
My fair lady.

Pease pudding hot,
Pease pudding cold,
Pease pudding in the pot,
Nine days old.

Teach the pupils 'London Bridge' and 'Pease pudding hot'. Divide the pupils into two groups to perform the songs at the same time.

Divide the pupils into three groups to try the two songs and the ostinato together.

Optional sung ostinato

Traditional

Briskly

Ten green bottles/Green glass partner songs

Ten green bottles hanging on the wall,
Ten green bottles hanging on the wall.
If one green bottle should
    accidentally fall,
There'll be nine green bottles
    hanging on the wall.

Nine green bottles ...

Eight green bottles ...

One green bottle ...

Fancy leaving bottles a-hanging
    on the wall,
You don't need to be a genius to
    know they're going to fall.
So take them for recycling to the
    special bin.
Just listen to the smashes as you
    drop them in.

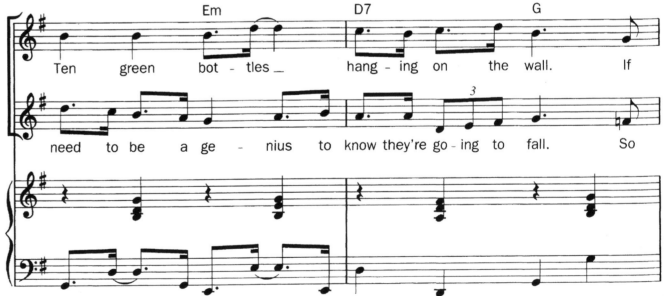

'Ten green bottles': *Traditional*
'Green glass': *Words and music by Sue Nicholls*

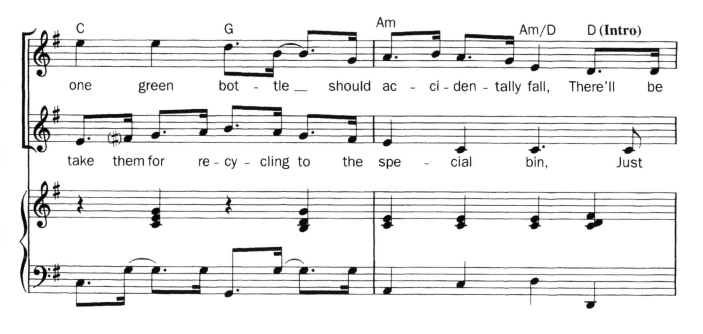

one green bot‑tle __ should ac‑ci‑den‑tally fall, There'll be

take them for re‑cy‑cling to the spe‑cial bin, Just

When the pupils can confidently sing 'Ten green bottles' and 'Green glass', divide the pupils into two groups to perform the songs as partner songs.

These partner songs can sound successful with or without the piano accompaniment.

nine green bot‑tles __ hang‑ing on the wall.

lis‑ten to the sma‑shes as you drop them in.

53

Alleluia amen/Michael, row the boat ashore

partner songs

We sing alleluia, alleluia,
Alleluia, amen.
We sing alleluia, sing alleluia,
Alleluia, amen.

Michael, row the boat ashore,
  Alleluia,
Michael, row the boat ashore,
  Alleluia.

Sister help to trim the sail,
  Alleluia ...

Brother won't you lend a hand,
  Alleluia,
Steer this boat to the Promised Land,
  Alleluia.

Michael, row the boat ashore,
  Alleluia ...

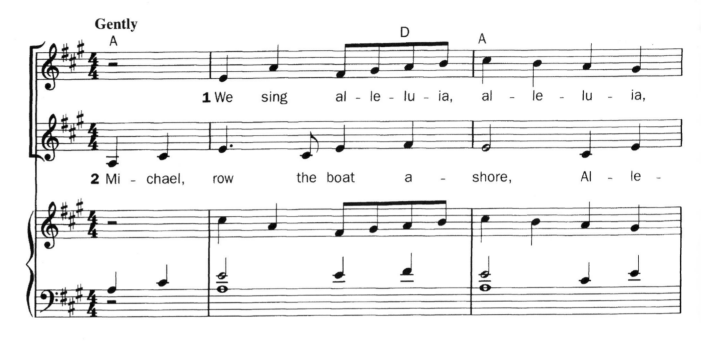

'Alleluia amen': Words and music by Sue Nicholls
'Michael, row the boat ashore': Traditional

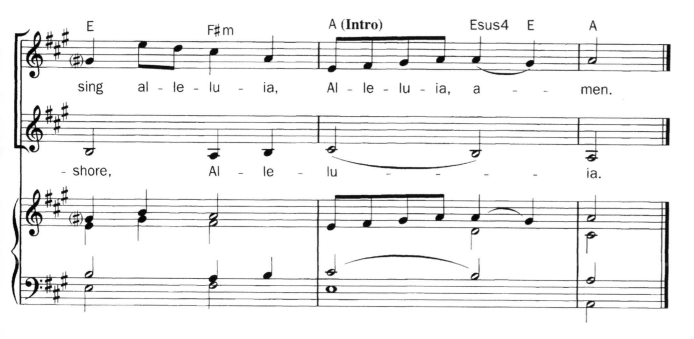

When the pupils can confidently sing 'Alleluia amen' and 'Michael, row the boat ashore', divide the pupils into two groups to sing both songs together as partner songs.

These partner songs sound successful with or without the piano accompaniment.

Partner syllables a listening game

One pupil is chosen to be the listener; he or she leaves the room. Everyone else sits in a circle.

Choose a word with two syllables, such as 'singer'. The teacher allocates the two syllables so that half of the pupils have 'sing-', and the other half have '-er'.

Choose a well-known tune such as 'Here we go Looby Loo'.

The listener is invited back into the room. Starting all together (e.g. after a count of four), everyone in the circle sings the well-known tune with his or her syllable sound. The listener has to work out what the original word was.

To make this game harder, choose a word with three syllables.

Contributed by Helen MacGregor

God bless the master

a song with partner verses

Verse 1

God bless the master of this house,
The mistress also,
And all the little children
    that round the table go.

Verse 2

And all your kin and kinsfolk,
That dwell both far and near,
We wish you a merry Christmas,
    And a happy new year.

Optional alternative words for last two lines:
We wish you good health and happiness,
Each and every year.

Divide the pupils into two groups and follow
this performance guide:
1 Verse 1 Verse 2 Verse 1 Verse 2 Verse 1 Verse 2
2 Verse 1 Verse 2 Silence Verse 1 Verse 2 Verse 1

English traditional words
Music by Malcolm Abbs

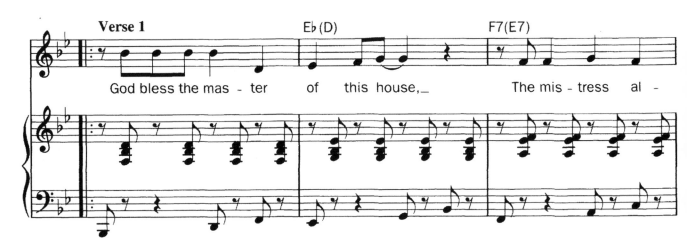

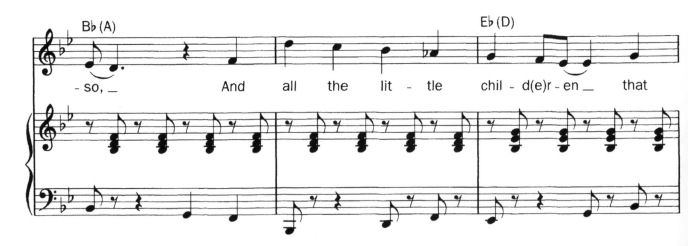

56

Mum and Dads — a song with partner verses

1+2 Chorus
Mums and Dads, Mums and Dads,
Let's play Mums and Dads,
Mums and Dads, Mums and Dads,
Funny Mums and Dads.

1 'Mum'
Where you been all night?
    Yes, your dinner's on the light,
Don't consider poor me just as
    long as you're alright,
Johnny wants new shoes and the
    kids have bust a fuse,
And you really do look a sight!

2 'Dad'
I bumped into Charlie Brown,
Remember Charlie Brown?
    Good old Charlie Brown.
When he said 'Let's paint the town',
I couldn't let an old friend down.

Divide the pupils into two groups and follow
this performance guide:

| **1** | Chorus | Mum | Silence | Chorus | Mum |
| **2** | Chorus | Silence | Dad | Chorus | Dad |

Words and music by Lionel Bart

58

long as you're al-right, John - ny wants new shoes, and the kids have bust a fuse, And you real - ly do look a

sight! **2** I bumped in - to Char - lie Brown, Re - mem - ber Char - lie Brown? Good old Char - lie Brown.

When he said, 'Let's paint the town', I could - n't let an old friend down!

Wipe, sniff, drip
a song with independent parts

1 When you have a cold,
2 When you have a cold,
1 Then your nose is raw,
2 Then your nose is raw,
1 Head begins to ache,
2 Head begins to ache,
1 And your throat is sore,
2 And your throat is sore.

1 Chorus
Wipe, wipe,
   sniffle,
Wipe, wipe,
   sniffle,
Drip, drip,
   atchoo!

2 Chorus
Wipe, sniffle,
   wipe,
Wipe, sniffle,
   wipe,
Drip, drip,
   atchoo!

1 Then you lose your voice,
2 Then you lose your voice,
1 It becomes a wheeze,
2 It becomes a wheeze,
1 Followed by a cough,
2 Followed by a cough,
1 After every sneeze,
2 After every sneeze.

Chorus

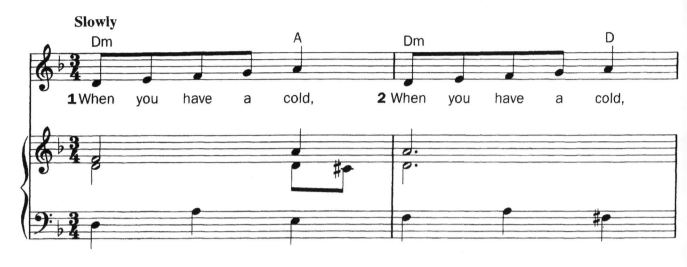

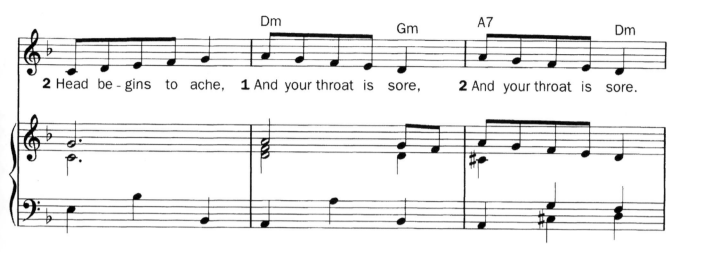

1 Think of wicked things,
2 Think of wicked things,
1 You would like to do,
2 You would like to do,
1 To the friend who gave,
2 To the friend who gave,
1 All those germs to you,
2 All those germs to you.

Chorus

Divide the pupils into two groups to perform the verse as an echo and the chorus in two parts.

Make up actions to go with 'wipe', 'sniffle', 'drip' and 'achoo' to perform when you sing the chorus.

This song works well without the piano accompaniment.

Words and music by Sue Nicholls

I wanna sing scat

a song with independent parts

1

I wanna sing scat,
   sing scat,
I wanna sing scat,
   sing scat,
I wanna sing scat,
   sing scat,
I wanna sing scat,
   sing scat,
   sing scat.

I wanna sing bop ...

I wanna sing swing ...

I wanna sing jazz ...

I wanna sing scat ...

2

Cool cat,
   cool cat,
Cool cat,
   cool cat,
Cool cat,
   cool cat,
Cool cat,
   sing scat,
   cool cat.

Be bop ...

Ring-a-ding ...

Jazza-ma-tazz ...

Cool cat ...

Words and music by Malcolm Abbs

Gm(Em)

wan - na sing scat, sing scat, sing scat. I scat, sing scat.

Cool cat, cool cat. cool cat.

1. - 4
D7(B7) Gm(Em)

5.
D7(B7) Gm(Em)

Divide the pupils into two groups to sing 'I wanna sing scat'. Make sure that each group can confidently perform its part before performing both parts together.

Hello...goodbye greetings in harmony

Divide the pupils into four groups. The pupils sing the notes of the C major chord, going upwards, for 'Hello'. You start each group one at a time and stop them together.

The children sing the same notes going downwards, for 'Goodbye'. You start and stop each group as before.

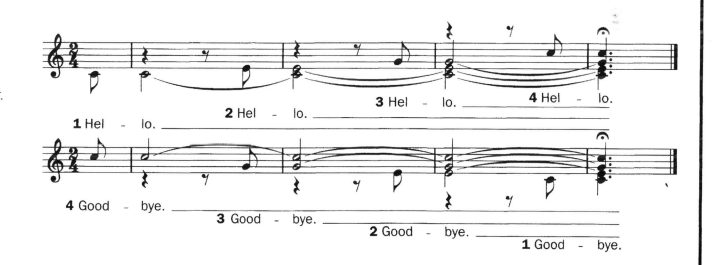

1 Hel - lo. ___
2 Hel - lo. ___
3 Hel - lo. ___
4 Hel - lo.

4 Good - bye. ___
3 Good - bye. ___
2 Good - bye. ___
1 Good - bye.

Contributed by Helen MacGregor

63

Swing low, sweet chariot
a song with a canon in the chorus

Chorus

Swing low, sweet chariot,
Comin' for to carry me home,
Swing low, sweet chariot,
Comin' for to carry me home.

Verse 1

I looked over Jordan and
      what did I see,
Comin' for to carry me home?
A band of angels comin' after me,
Comin' for to carry me home.

Chorus

Verse 2

If you get there before I do,
Comin' for to carry me home.
Tell all my friends I'm comin' too,
Comin' for to carry me home.

Traditional spiritual

Verse

Divide the pupils into two groups to perform the chorus as a canon.

In the verses, part 2 is an optional harmony line for a second group. The verses can be performed successfully with or without it.

Cat and mouse games
partner songs

1 Cats sleep anywhere,
Any table, any chair,
Top of piano, window ledge.
In the middle, on the edge,
Open drawer, empty shoe,
Anybody's lap will do,
Fitted in a cardboard box,
In the cupboard with your frocks.
Anywhere! They don't care!
Cats sleep anywhere. (CATS!)

2 Their tails are long, their faces
small,
They haven't any chins at all,
I think mice are rather nice.
Their ears are pink, their teeth
are white,
They run about the house at night,
I think mice are rather nice.
They nibble things they shouldn't
touch,
And no-one seems to like them
much.
But I think mice are nice! (MICE!)

'Cats': a poem by Eleanor Farjeon
'Mice': a poem by Rose Fyleman
Music by Malcolm Abbs

A - ny - bo - dy's lap will do, Fit - ted in a card - board __ box, _____

run a - bout the house at night. I think mice are

In the cup - board with your frocks. _____ A - ny where!__ They don't care!

ra - - ther nice. They nib - ble things they should - n't touch, And

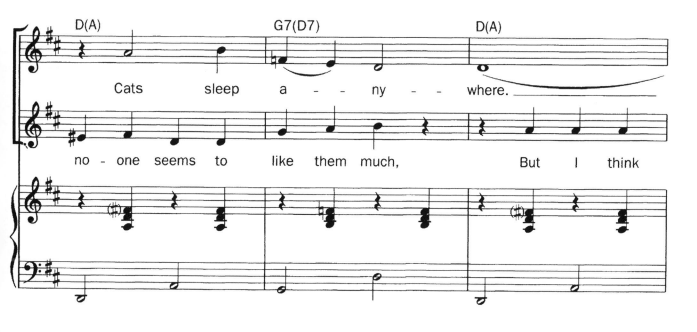

Cats sleep a — ny — — where.

no - one seems to like them much, But I think

Teach the two songs, then divide the pupils into two groups to sing both songs at the same time. Follow this performance guide:

1 Cats Silence Cats end
2 Silence Mice Mice end

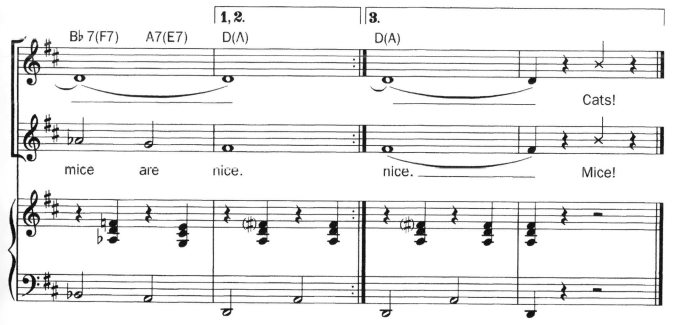

mice are nice. nice. ___ Cats!

             Mice!

Stand by me
a song with an ostinato accompaniment

2 Ostinato

Boom pe che boom, do do,

Boom pe che boom, do do ...

1 Verse 1

When the night has come,

And the land is dark,

And the moon is the only light we'll see.

No I won't be afraid,

No I won't be afraid,

Just as long as you stand, stand by me.

1+2 Chorus

So, darling, darling,

Stand by me, oh, stand by me,

Oh, stand, stand by me, stand by me.

1 Verse 2

If the sea that we look upon,

Should tumble and fall,

Or the mountain should crumble
   in the sea.

I won't cry, I won't cry,

No I won't shed a tear,

Just as long as you stand, stand by me.

1+2 Chorus

*Words and music by Ben E. King, Jerry Leiber
and Mike Stoller*

won't   be a-fraid, __   Just as long _____   as you stand, ____   stand by me.

boom pe che boom,   do do boom pe che boom,   do do boom pe che boom,   do do boom pe che boom,   do do

— So, dar-ling, dar-ling, Stand _____ by   me, oh, ____   stand _____ by

boom pe che boom,   So, dar-ling, dar-ling, Stand _____ by   me, oh, ____   stand _____ by

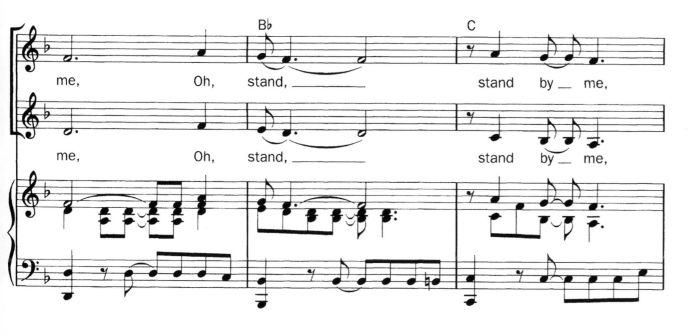

me,   Oh,   stand, _____   stand   by _ me,

me,   Oh,   stand, _____   stand   by _ me,

stand   by _ me. _____   If the sea ___

stand   by _ me. _____   Do do, ___

The ostinato part should be sung with a steady beat throughout. Make the 'pe che' sounds very gentle.

The melody line of this song is very syncopated and individual singers may want to vary the rhythm of the melody from that given in the music. However, if a group of pupils are singing part 1, make sure that they sing with the same rhythm.

This body percussion pattern can be performed with the song:

Body percussion pattern

tap   clap   click

El condor pasa

a song with a canon in the verse

I'd rather be a sparrow than a snail.
Yes I would, if I could,
I surely would, hm.
I'd rather be a hammer than a nail.
Yes I would, if I only could,
I surely would, hm.

Away, I'd rather sail away,
Like a swan that's here and gone.
A man gets tied up to the ground,
He gives the world its saddest sound,
Its saddest sound.

I'd rather be a forest than a street.
Yes I would, if I could,
I surely would.
I'd rather feel the earth beneath
my feet.
Yes I would, if I only could,
I surely would.

Away, I'd rather sail away ...

Music and words by Daniel Alomeas Robles and
Jorge Milchberg
English words by Paul Simon

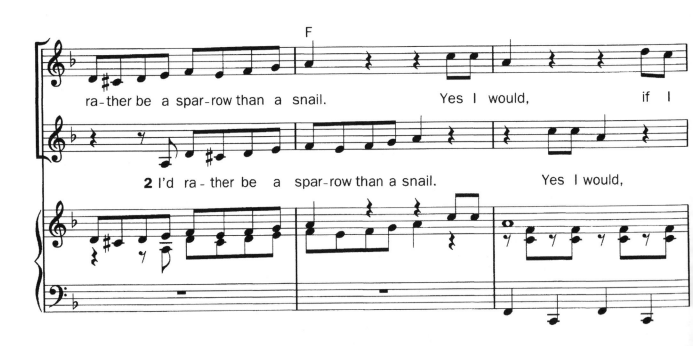

could,   I sure-ly would, __   hm. _____   I'd ra-ther be a ham-mer than a nail.   Yes I

if I could,   I sure-ly would, _   hm. _____   I'd ra-ther be a ham-mer than a nail.

would,   if I on-ly could, _____ I sure-ly would, _   hm. _____   A - way,   I'd ra-ther sail a-

Yes I would,   if I on-ly could, _____ I sure-ly would,   hm. _____ A - way,   I'd ra-ther sail a-

-way, ___ Like a swan that's here and gone. A man gets tied up to the ground, He gives the

-way, ___ Like a swan that's here and gone. A man gets tied up to the ground, He gives the

world its sad-dest sound, Its sad-dest sound. ___

world its sad-dest sound, Its sad-dest sound. ___

One, two, three, four

a song with four independent parts

1 This song has a melody you
  cannot ignore,
A solo so beautiful it needs
  nothing more.

2 If we add another line you will
  certainly find,
That singing together makes a
  duet quite divine.

3 But listen to our part and then
  you'll agree,
A trio brings harmony perfect
  for three.

4 A fine quartet you won't forget,
A fine quartet you won't forget.

Divide the pupils into four groups to sing 'One, two, three, four' as a four-part song. (If you wish to perform this song in three parts only, omit the fourth part.)

Follow this performance plan:

	1st time	2nd time	3rd time	4th time
1	Sing	Sing	Sing	Sing
2	Silence	Sing	Sing	Sing
3	Silence	Silence	Sing	Sing
4	Silence	Silence	Silence	Sing

Words and music by Sue Nicholls

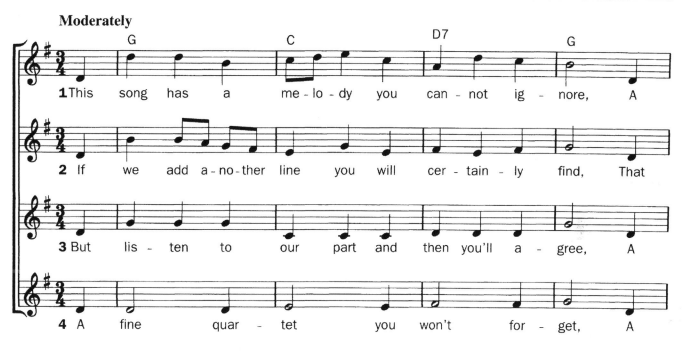

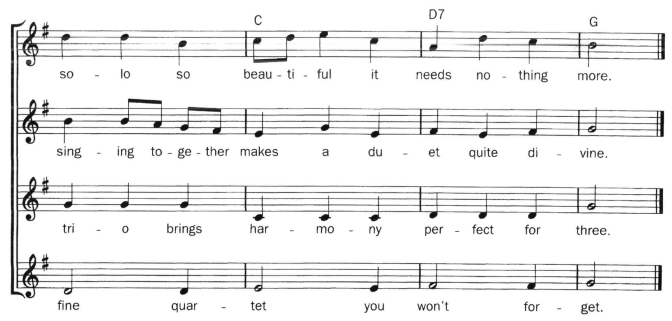

Souallé

an unaccompanied three-part lullaby

Souallé, souallé, souallé, souallé,
Souallé, souallé, souallé, souallé ...

Divide the pupils into three groups to perform
this three-part lullaby.

Traditional African

Acknowledgements

The following copyright owners have kindly granted their permission for the inclusion of these items:

Malcolm Abbs for the music of **Cat and mouse games, God bless the master, How doth the little crocodile** and the music and words of **I wanna sing scat** and **Noah's shanty,** © 1995 Malcolm Abbs.

Mr Peter Combe for **Mister Clicketty Cane** © Mr Peter Combe PO Box 146 Glenside South Australia 5065. All Rights Reserved.

EMI United Partnership Ltd, London for **Mums and Dads**. Words and music by Lionel Bart © 1962 EMI United Partnership Ltd. Worldwide Print rights controlled by Warner Bros Publications Inc/IMP Ltd. Reproduced by permission of IMP Ltd. All Rights Reserved.

Christopher Green for the words of **Tongo** and the words of **Emanuel** (translated by Peter Honniball), Source Colony Holidays repertoire.

David Higham Associates for **Cats** by Eleanor Farjeon from *The Children's Bells* © 1957.

Edward Kassner Music Co Ltd for **Choo choo (I gotta hurry home)** by Bob Schafer, Duke Ellington and Dave Ringler. © 1927 Broadway Music Corporation for the World. All Rights Reserved. By permission of Edward Kassner Music Co Ltd.

Nancy Kerr for contributing the traditional **The shark.**

Hal Leonard Corporation for **Stand by me**. Words and music by Ben E King, Jerry Leiber and Mike Stoller. © 1961 (renewed) Jerry Leiber Music, Mike Stoller Music and Trio Music Company Inc. All Rights Reserved.

Sue Lubner and Tamar Swade for the words of **Ewe!**, © 1995.

Edward B Marks Music Corporation and Jorge Milchberg for **El Condor Pasa (If I could)**. English lyric by Paul Simon. Musical arrangement by Jorge Milchberg and Daniel Robles. Copyright © 1933, 1963, 1970 by Edward B Marks Music Corporation and Jorge Milchberg. English lyric © 1970 (renewed) by Paul Simon. International copyright secured. All Rights Reserved. Reprinted by permission of Music Sales Corporation.

Sue Nicholls for **The band, Alleluia amen/Michael row the boat, Ten green bottles/Green glass, Wipe, sniff, drip** and **One, two, three, four**, © 1995 Sue Nicholls.

Random House Inc for **Mice**, from *Fifty-one New Nursery Rhymes* by Rose Fyleman, copyright 1931, 1932 by Doubleday, a division of Random House Inc. Used by permission of Random House Children's Books, a division of Random House Inc.

Ana Sanderson for **Banana Splits, Tomorrow's another day, Fiddle diddle, The green cross code, Sports day race** and **The human drum kit** © 1995 Ana Sanderson.

Schott & Co Ltd for **I hear the bells** © 1984 Schott & Co Ltd, this arrangement © 1994 Schott & Co Ltd. Reproduced by permission. Also for **TV tantrum** © 1984 Schott & Co Ltd. Reproduced by permission. All Rights Reserved.

Scott Prentice for **Rings and circles** by Jan Harmon. © reprinted by permission.

Simon & Schuster for **Sing a little song** by Henry E Dennis, Jr from *Silver Burdett Music, Early Childhood* © 1981 by Silver Burdett Ginn, Simon & Schuster Elementary. Used by permission.

The Society of Authors as the United Kingdom and Canadian literary representative of Rose Fyleman for **Mice** by Rose Fyleman.

Tamar Swade for the music of **Jelly on a plate** and **Ewe!** © 1995 Tamar Swade.

Kaye Umansky C/O Caroline Sheldon Literary Agency for the words of **Big Ben Bean and his joke machine** and **Poppycock pie**, © 1995. Used by kind permission.

Grateful acknowledgement is made to the following who have advised or helped in compiling this collection of songs, chants and games: Malcolm Abbs, John Bannister, Shashi Joshi and family, Ronald Joyce, Gillyanne Kayes, Sandra Kerr, Emma Killick, Helen MacGregor, Sue Nicholls, Sheena Roberts, Jane Sebba, Tamar Swade, Angela Tilly and David Vinden.

Accompaniments for **God bless the master, I wanna sing scat** and **Cat and mouse games** arranged by Malcolm Abbs. Other accompaniments arranged by Ana Sanderson.

Index of first lines and titles